Cool Hotels
Spain

teNeues

Imprint

Produced by fusion publishing GmbH, Stuttgart . Los Angeles   www.fusion-publishing.com

Editorial team: Martin Nicholas Kunz (Editor + Layout)
Haike Falkenberg (Introduction), Jake Townsend ("What's special" texts)
Viviana Guastalla, Hanna Martin (Editorial coordination)
Sabine Scholz (Text coordination), Alphagriese (Translation coordination)
Dr. Elisabetta Sangirardi (Italian), Christine Grimm (US-English), Stéphanie Laloix (French), Juan Francisco Lopez (Spanish)
Jan Hausberg, Anke Scholz (Prepress + imaging)

Cover photo (location): Roger Mendez (Hotel San Roque)

Back cover photos from top to bottom (location): courtesy Hospes Hotels & Moments (Hospes Palacio del Bailío), courtesy Hospes Hotels & Moments (Hospes Las Casas del Rey de Baeza), courtesy B-Hotel, Joserra Santamaría (Miró Hotel), courtesy Mas de Torrent Hotel & Spa

Photos (location): courtesy Barcelona Catedral; courtesy B-Hotel; courtesy Casa Fuster; Albert Font (Ses Pitreras); courtesy Grand Hotel Central; courtesy Habitat Hotels (NERI Hotel & Restaurante); courtesy Hospedería La Parra; courtesy Hospes Hotels & Moments (Hospes Maricel, Hospes Palacio del Bailío, Hospes Palacio de los Patos, Hospes Las Casas del Rey de Baeza, Hospes Villa Paulita, Hospes Amérigo, Hospes Palau de la Mar); courtesy Hotel Hacienda Na Xamena (Hotel Hacienda Na Xamena p. 127); courtesy Hotel Marqués de Riscal, *The Luxury Collection* (Hotel Marqués de Riscal); courtesy Hotel Pulitzer; Jordi Miralles (Hotel Soho Barcelona pp. 84–87); Jörg Tietje (Son Gener); Joserra Santamaría (Miró Hotel); Katharina Feuer (El Hotel Pacha, Hotel Hacienda Na Xamena pp. 124–126, 128–129); courtesy Mas de Torrent Hotel & Spa; Matthias Nero (Puro); Michelle Galindo (Hotel Soho Barcelona pp. 88–89, Market Hotel pp. 90–91); courtesy Portixol; courtesy Posada La Sacristía; Rafael Vargas (Hotel Omm); Roger Mendez (Hotel San Roque); courtesy Son Brull Hotel & Spa; courtesy The Beach House; Wain Chasan (exteriores El Juncal), Jane Monroe (interiores El Juncal); Xavier Barbarro (Axel Hotel Barcelona)
All other photos by Martin Nicholas Kunz

Price orientation: € < 200 EUR, €€ 201–350 EUR, €€€ 351–550 EUR, €€€€ > 551 EUR

Published by teNeues Publishing Group

teNeues Verlag GmbH + Co. KG
Am Selder 37
47906 Kempen, Germany
Tel.: 0049-(0)2152-916-0
Fax: 0049-(0)2152-916-111
E-mail: books@teneues.de

teNeues Publishing Company
16 West 22nd Street
New York, NY 10010, USA
Tel.: 001-212-627-9090
Fax: 001-212-627-9511

teNeues Publishing UK Ltd.
P.O. Box 402
West Byfleet
KT14 7ZF, Great Britain
Tel.: 0044-1932-403509
Fax: 0044-1932-403514

teNeues France S.A.R.L.
93, rue Bannier
45000 Orléans, France
Tel.: 0033-2-38541071
Fax: 0033-2-38625340

Press department: arehn@teneues.de
Tel.: 0049-(0)2152-916-202

www.teneues.com

ISBN: 978-3-8327-9230-5

Bibliographic information published by Die Deutsche Bibliothek.
Die Deutsche Bibliothek lists this publication in the Deutsche Nationalbibliografie;
detailed bibliographic data is available in the Internet at http://dnb.ddb.de.

Contents   Page

Introducción

Caso de creer los eslóganes de la Oficina de Turismo de España, entonces "España es diferente", ofrece "todo bajo el sol" y, una vez allí, lo que uno se dice es: "¡Sonríe! Estás en España". Tres verdades estas sobre las que merece la pena profundizar.

En primer lugar, España es verdaderamente diferente. La diversidad cultural de este país desafía a la globalización y al ingente número de turistas, al tiempo que asimila las influencias externas con una sorprendente naturalidad. Hasta tal punto que un término muy de moda entre la *jet set* internacional como es "cool" no se ha instaurado en el vocabulario hispano.

Lo mismo ocurre con los hoteles presentados en este volumen: son "diferentes". Como ejemplo está el *Hotel Marqués de Riscal*. En este hotel de la región vitivinícola de La Rioja, cualquiera puede cumplir su sueño de dormir bajo la sinuosa techumbre obra de Frank O. Gehry. Y en Madrid, un total de 19 arquitectos y diseñadores de primera línea han conseguido crear con el *Hotel Silken Puerta América* un singular mundo de sensaciones, mundo que la palabra "hotel" se queda corta al describir.

En segundo lugar, el sol brilla con tanta frecuencia en estas tierras –algo envidiable en otras latitudes– que las casas más modernas de la Ciudad Condal se han construido consecuentemente con terrazas en las azoteas, desde las que los huéspedes, tendidos en tumbonas de diseño, disfrutan de las vistas a la ciudad, al interior o al mar, degustan platos innovadores o se refrescan en piscinas llenas de estilo. Junto a estos elegantes templos urbanos de la hospitalidad, existe una amplia oferta de hoteles rurales a la última. En su gran mayoría, el mobiliario interior está dominado por el carácter minimalista y la aplicación de colores es especialmente escasa. El blanco tradicional de las casas encaladas del sur de España cubre principalmente las paredes de las estancias –aunque no solo estas– mientras que en los cuartos de baño, caso de estar separados del dormitorio, predominan los translúcidos.

Y en tercer lugar, cuando uno tiene a sus pies toda una ciudad, como sucede en el caso del *Gran Hotel La Florida*, o se tiene la sensación de ocupar en solitario toda el ala de la impresionante al tiempo que sencilla casa de campo *Son Gener;* o cuando en la terraza del *Hotel Hacienda Na Xamena* se disfruta de las cálidas aguas de un hidromasaje mientras la vista se relaja contemplando la escarpada costa ibicenca y el azul del mar, entonces no queda más remedio que sonreír, sonreír y nada más que sonreír.

Haike Falkenberg

Introduction

If you believe the advertising slogans of the Spanish tourist association, then "Spain is simply different." It offers "everything under the sun." And once you arrive there, you just have to "smile because you are in Spain." These are three truths that deserve to be explored.

First: Spain really is different. The varied Spanish cultures defy globalization and the floods of tourists by assimilating foreign influences with an impressive matter-of-factness. Even "cool," the trendy word of the international jetsetters has yet to enter the Spanish language. And so the hotels presented in this book are "simply different." For example, the *Hotel Marqués de Riscal*. This hotel in the winegrowing area of Rioja makes it possible for anyone to fulfill the dream of sleeping under the sweeping roof of a structure built by Frank O. Gehry. And a total of 19 star architects and designers have created a unique experiential world in Madrid with the *Hotel Silken Puerta América* that is inadequately described by the word "hotel."

Second: The sun shines so enviably often and long there that the most modern houses of the Catalan capital of Barcelona now set up rooftop terraces as a matter of course. Guests can look out at the city, country, and sea from designer loungers, enjoy the innovative cuisine, or refresh themselves in a stylish swimming pool. In addition to these chic temples of hospitality in the metropolises, there is a large variety of trendy country hotels. What almost all of them have in common is that their interior design is dominated by minimalist furniture and colors are used extremely sparingly. Above all, the traditional white of the whitewashed houses in the south of Spain covers the walls of the rooms—and more. On the other hand, transparency dominates in the bathrooms, if they are separated at all from the sleeping area.

And third: When the entire city lies at your feet, as in the case of the *Gran Hotel La Florida*, you have the feeling of living alone in an entire wing of the breathtakingly simple country house *Son Gener*; or when you soak in the warm water of the whirlpool on one of the terraces of the *Hotel Hacienda Na Xamena* while your eyes gaze over Ibiza's rugged coast and the blue sea—then you can only do one thing: smile, smile, smile.

Haike Falkenberg

Einleitung

Glaubt man den Werbesprüchen des spanischen Fremdenverkehrsvereins, dann „ist Spanien einfach anders". Es biete „alles unter der Sonne" und einmal dort angekommen, müsse man einfach „lächeln, denn man ist in Spanien". Drei Wahrheiten, denen auf den Grund zu gehen lohnt.

Erstens: Spanien ist wirklich anders. Die vielfältigen spanischen Kulturen trotzen Globalisierung und Touristenströmen, indem sie fremde Einflüsse mit beeindruckender Selbstverständlichkeit assimilieren. Sogar das Trendwort der internationalen Jetsetter, „cool", fand bislang keinen Eingang in die spanische Sprache. Und so sind auch die Hotels, die in diesem Buch vorgestellt werden, „einfach anders". Zum Beispiel das *Hotel Marqués de Riscal*. In diesem Hotel im Weinanbaugebiet Rioja kann sich jeder den Traum erfüllen, ein Mal unter dem schwungvollen Dach eines Bauwerks von Frank O. Gehry zu schlafen. Und in Madrid haben insgesamt 19 Stararchitekten und -designer mit dem *Hotel Silken Puerta América* eine einzigartige Erlebniswelt gestaltet, die mit dem Wort Hotel nur unzureichend beschrieben wird.

Zweitens: Die Sonne scheint dort so beneidenswert oft und lange, dass die modernsten Häuser der katalanischen Hauptstadt Barcelona mit neuer Selbstverständlichkeit Dachterrassen eingerichtet haben, auf denen die Gäste von Designerliegen aus auf Stadt, Land und Meer blicken, die innovative Küche genießen oder sich in einem stilvollen Schwimmbad erfrischen können. Neben diesen chicen Tempeln der Gastlichkeit in den Metropolen gibt es eine große Vielfalt an trendigen Landhotels. Fast allen ist gemein, dass in ihren Inneneinrichtungen minimalistische Möbel dominieren und die Farben äußerst sparsam eingesetzt werden. Das traditionelle Weiß der gekalkten Häuser Südspaniens bedeckt vor allem – aber nicht nur – die Zimmerwände, während bei den Badezimmern, wenn sie überhaupt vom Schlafraum abgetrennt sind, Transparenz vorherrscht.

Und drittens: Wenn einem wie im Fall des *Gran Hotel La Florida* eine ganze Stadt zu Füßen liegt, man das Gefühl hat, gleich einen ganzen Flügel des atemberaubend schlichten Landhauses *Son Gener* alleine zu bewohnen oder auf einer der Terrassen des *Hotel Hacienda Na Xamena* im warmen Wasser des Whirlpools liegt, während die Augen über die schroffe Küste Ibizas und das blaue Meer blicken – dann kann man nur eins: lächeln, lächeln, lächeln.

Haike Falkenberg

Introduction

A en croire les slogans de l'Office du Tourisme d'Espagne, « L'Espagne est tout simplement différente », vous offre « tout sous le soleil » et, une fois là-bas, vous vous dites : « Souriez ! Vous êtes en Espagne ». Ce sont trois vérités qui méritent d'être approfondies. Premièrement, l'Espagne est vraiment différente. La diversité culturelle de ce pays défie la mondialisation et les hordes de touristes en assimilant les influences externes avec un naturel surprenant. Au point qu'un mot aussi répandu dans la jet-set internationale que « cool » n'est pas entré dans le vocabulaire espagnol.

Cela vaut aussi pour les hôtels présentés dans cet ouvrage, ils sont « tout simplement différents », comme le *Hotel Marqués de Riscal*, par exemple. Dans cet hôtel de la région vinicole de la Rioja, n'importe qui peut réaliser son rêve en dormant sous le plafond sinueux d'une structure œuvre de Frank O. Gehry. Et à Madrid, un groupe de 19 architectes et designers de premier plan se sont réunis pour créer au sein de l'*Hotel Silken Puerta América* un monde singulier de sensations, monde que le mot « hôtel » ne peut définir totalement. Deuxièmement, le soleil brille si souvent sous ces latitudes (ce qu'on envie ailleurs), que les hôtels les plus modernes de Barcelone, la capitale catalane, disposent tout naturellement de terrasses de toits, sur lesquelles les hôtes, affalés sur des chaises longues de designer, profitent de la vue sur la ville ou sur la mer, dégustent des plats innovants ou se rafraîchissent dans des piscines de style. Outre ces temples urbains de l'hôtellerie, il existe une vaste offre d'élégants hôtels ruraux. Ils partagent souvent un point commun : un design intérieur dominé par le minimalisme et une utilisation particulièrement parcimonieuse des couleurs. Et surtout, le blanc traditionnel des maisons chaulées du sud de l'Espagne couvre, entre autres, les murs des salles de séjour, alors que la transparence domine dans les salles de bains – si elles sont séparées de la chambre.

Et troisièmement, quand vous avez à vos pieds toute la ville, comme à la *Gran Hotel La Florida*, ou que vous avez l'impression d'occuper seul toute une aile de l'impressionnante mais simple maison de campagne *Son Gener*, ou que vous vous détendez dans les eaux chaudes d'un bain bouillonnant sur la terrasse de l'*Hotel Hacienda Na Xamena* tout en profitant de la vue sur la côte escarpée d'Ibiza et le bleu profond de la mer, il ne vous reste plus qu'une chose à faire : sourire, sourire et encore sourire.

Haike Falkenberg

Introduzione

Se si crede ai detti pubblicitari delle proloco turistiche spagnole, allora "la Spagna è semplicemente diversa". Offre "tutto sotto il sole" e una volta giunti sul posto si deve semplicemente "sorridere perché ci si trova in Spagna". Tre verità, sulle quali vale la pena indagare. Primo: la Spagna è veramente diversa. Le svariate culture spagnole resistono alla globalizzazione e alle masse di turisti, assimilando le influenze straniere con una naturalezza impressionante. Anche la parola trend del jetset internazionale "cool", non ha trovato fino ad ora accesso alla lingua spagnola. E così anche gli hotel, che vengono presentati in questo libro, sono "semplicemente diversi". Per esempio il *Hotel Marqués de Riscal*. In questo hotel, posto nel paesaggio di viticoltura Rioja, ognuno può trasformare in realtà il sogno di dormire sotto il tetto slanciato di una costruzione di Frank O. Gehry. E a Madrid 19 architetti e designer di fama mondiale hanno allestito un mondo unico di esperienza con il *Hotel Silken Puerta América*, che viene descritto in modo assolutamente insufficiente dalla parola hotel.

Secondo: il sole splende in modo così invidiabilmente frequente in questo paese che i palazzi più moderni della capitale catalana Barcellona hanno allestito dei terrazzi sui tetti. Da questi terrazzi gli ospiti possono godere della vista sulla città, sulla campagna e sul mare, sdraiati su lettini di design, gustare la cucina innovativa oppure rinfrescarsi nella piscina allestita con stile. Vicino a questi templi chic dedicati alla ospitalità, situati nelle metropoli, esiste una grande varietà di hotel di campagna alla moda. Al loro interno dominano nella maggior parte dei casi allestimenti con mobili minimalistici e colori usati in modo parsimonioso. Il bianco tradizionale delle case tinte in calce, tipiche del sud della Spagna, copre soprattutto – ma non solo – le pareti delle stanze, mentre nei bagni, sempre che siano divisi dalle camere da letto, domina la trasparenza.

E terzo: se come nel caso del *Gran Hotel La Florida* si ha tutta la città ai propri piedi, se si ha la sensazione di avere a disposizione da soli addirittura un'intera ala della semplice casa di campagna *Son Gener*, bella da togliere il fiato, oppure se si sta sdraiati nell'acqua calda di una vasca idromassaggio su una delle terrazze del *Hotel Hacienda Na Xamena*, mentre gli occhi scorrono sulla costa scoscesa di Ibiza e il mare azzurro – allora si può solo fare una cosa: sorridere, sorridere, sorridere.

Haike Falkenberg

9

Hospes Palacio del Bailío

Ramírez de las Casas de Deza,
10–12
14001 Córdoba
Andalucía
Phone: +34 957 498 993
Fax: +34 957 498 994
www.hospes.com

Price category: €€
Rooms: 50 rooms, 2 suites and 1 big loft suite
Facilities: Senzone restaurant, tapas bar, lounge bar, Bodyna spa, massage & treatments, pool and roman baths
Services: Meeting rooms for up to 120 people
Located: in the city center, next to the Cristo de los Faroles statue
Map: No. 1
Style: Cultural Heritage Building
What's special: Once a grand working palace, this 17th century building is now host to a charming oasis of luxury and peace in the heart of Córdoba. Each room is stylish and minimal. The spa utilizes ancient treatments in one of the most beautiful settings in Spain.

Posada La Sacristía

San Donato, 8
11380 Tarifa
Andalucía
Phone: +34 956 681 795
Fax: +34 956 685 182
www.lasacristia.net

Price category: €€€€
Rooms: 10 rooms
Facilities: Horseback riding, kite and windsurfing instructors, boat trips for whale and dolphin watching
Services: Therapeutic massages
Located: 35 minutes to Tangier
Map: No. 2
Style: Modern countrystyle
What's special: Like something from another time, this 10 room hotel is among the best kept secrets in Spain. Decorated in a minimal, yet elegant palette, there is a world class restaurant and bar, and some of the best windsurfing in Spain right around the corner.

Posada La Sacristía

Hospes Palacio de los Patos

Solarillo de Gracia, 1
18002 Granada
Andalucía
Phone: +34 958 535 790
Fax: +34 958 536 968
www.hospes.com

Price category: €€
Rooms: 42 rooms including 5 suites
Facilities: Senzone restaurant, Bodyna spa, massage &
treatments, pool, jacuzzi, sauna and turkish bath
Services: Meeting rooms for up to 60 people
Located: in the historic and business center of Granada
Map: No. 3
Style: Modern and 19th century contrasts
What's special: This former palace is now one of Grana-
da's most intriguing boutique hotels. The spectacular
19th century building has been transformed into a grand
palace for the 21st century by combining it with a new
design building with an impressive alabaster façade. Each
room is a balance of contemporary and classical, each with
plasma televisions, large bathrooms and free internet. The
Arabian garden is a great place to find a quiet moment.

Hospes Palacio de los Patos   23

29400 Ronda
Andalucía
Phone: +34 952 161 170
Fax: +34 952 161 160
www.eljuncal.com

Rooms: 11 rooms including 3 suites and 2 apartments
Facilities: Restaurant, bar, swimming pool, spa, sauna, wine therapy massages
Services: Winery
Located: a short drive to the center of Ronda, 1 hour to Málaga airport and 45 minutes to the beach
Map: No. 4
Style: Modern
What's special: Filled with art and furnishings by Philippe Starck, El Juncal has surprises around every corner. Each of the rooms has parquet floors and over-sized marble tubs. The suites are two-storied, some with private terraces and balconies.

Hospes Las Casas del Rey de Baeza

Santiago, 2
Plaza Jesus De La Redención
41003 Sevilla
Andalucía
Phone: +34 954 561 496
Fax: +34 954 561 441
www.hospes.com

Price category: €€
Rooms: 41 rooms including 5 suites
Facilities: Senzone restaurant (contemporary Andalusian cuisine), Senzone pool bar, Bodyna massages & treatments, Bodyna pool
Services: Meeting rooms for up to 60 people
Located: in the historical center of Sevilla, 10 km to Sevilla airport
Map: No. 5
Style: Andalusian character
What's special: As the only hotel in the area with a swimming pool on its roof, Las Casas del Rey de Baeza has one of the best views of the city. Most guest rooms have private balconies and marble bathrooms.

Axel Hotel Barcelona

Aribau, 33
08011 Barcelona
Eixample
Phone: +34 933 239 393
Fax: +34 933 239 394
www.axelhotels.com

Price category: €
Rooms: 66 rooms
Facilities: "Sky bar", lounge, spa, boutique
Services: Conference room for up to 100 people
Located: in walking distance from Las Ramblas, the
Gothic district and Plaza Catalunya
Public transportation: Metro Universitat, Passeig de Gràcia
Map: No. 6
Style: Modern
What's special: Named one of the 53 places to go in
2008 by the New York Times, Axel Hotel is the premier
gay hotel in Barcelona. Luxury suites include living rooms
and hydromassage bathtubs. From May until September,
the outdoor "Axel Sky Bar" is a popular spot for people
watching. Gay guests can register for the "Wild Weekend"
which grants VIP access to the best gay clubs in the city.

Banys Orientals

Calle Argenteria, 37
08003 Barcelona
El Born
Phone: +34 932 688 460
Fax: +34 932 688 461
www.hotelbanysorientals.com

Price category: €
Rooms: 43 rooms
Facilities: Catalan restaurant "Senyor Parellada"
Located: near the Cathedral and the Gothic district
Public transportation: Metro Yellow Jaume I
Map: No. 7
Style: Elegant
What's special: The historic building belies the bright modern guest rooms, each decorated in a cool, contemporary palette. The newly opened suites buildings, just a few steps away, offer guests elegant privacy in a loft-like setting.

Barcelona Catedral

Carrer dels Capellans, 4
08002 Barcelona
Ciutat Vella
Phone: +34 933 042 255
Fax: +34 933 042 366
www.barcelonacatedral.com

Price category: €€
Rooms: 80 rooms
Facilities: "4 Capellans Restaurant", bar, chill out area, terrace, pool, gym, meeting and banquet rooms
Services: Free internet and WiFi, parking, personal training
Located: in the very heart of Barcelona's historic quarter
Public transportation: Metro Yellow Jaume I, Metro Red & Green Catalunya
Map: No. 8
Style: Modern
What's special: Set in Barcelona's historic quarter, this hotel is a contemporary oasis. Besides a cutting edge Mediterranean cuisine, the restaurant offers cooking lessons and cooking team building. Two promenades are offered for free to the hotel guests: secrets and legends of the gothic quarter.

B-Hotel

Gran Vía, 389
08015 Barcelona
Eixample
Phone: +34 935 529 500
Fax: +34 935 529 501
www.nnhotels.com

Price category: €
Rooms: 84 rooms
Facilities: B-Bar, B-Cellar, terrace with pool and solarium
Services: Conference rooms for up to 80 people
Located: at Plaza Espanya next to sights and shopping areas. Nearby are Barcelona Fira and the Palau de Congresos Convention Centre
Public transportation: Metro Red & Green Espanya
Map: No. 9
Style: Urban
What's special: Built on the famed Plaza Espanya, B-Hotel has set the standard for lodging in Barcelona. Its rooftop infinity edge pool and solarium offers some of the best views of the city. The B-Bar is a great place to grab a drink before heading out into the city, day or evening.

Casa Fuster

Passeig de Gràcia, 132
08008 Barcelona
Eixample
Phone: +34 932 553 000
Fax: +34 932 553 002
www.hotelcasafuster.com

Price category: €€€
Rooms: 75 rooms, 21 suites
Facilities: "Restaurant Galaxó", "Café Vienés", rooftop pool, jacuzzi
Services: 10 meeting rooms for up to 300 people
Located: at the highest point of Passeig de Gràcia
Public transportation: Metro Green, Blue Diagonal
Map: No. 10
Style: Mixture of Art-Déco and traditional furnishing
What's special: This luxury hotel has long been on the list of top hotels in Spain. Originally a private residence, the building was the most expensive mansion in Barcelona when completed in 1911. The hotel now has two restaurants, a rooftop pool and jacuzzi and the "Café Vienés", situated on the ground floor, just steps away from the world famous Passeig de Gràcia.

Gran Hotel La Florida

Carretera Vallvidrera al
Tibidabo, 83–93
08035 Barcelona
Phone: +34 932 593 000
Fax: +34 932 593 001
www.hotellaflorida.com

Price category: €€
Rooms: 50 rooms, 12 suites, 8 design suites
Facilities: Gourmet restaurant, outdoor terrace bar, lobby lounge bar, indoor and outdoor pool, "ZenZone Spa", massage, meeting rooms with natural daylight
Services: Shuttle service to city center of Barcelona
Located: in the hills of Collserola with breathtaking view over Barcelona and the Mediterranean Sea
Map: No. 11
Style: Urban resort
What's special: Thanks to its privileged position dominating the city from an altitude of 512 meters, the Gran Hotel La Florida is regarded as a top luxury urban resort. In an incomparable setting, imbued with history, it offers guests the opportunity to live a Mediterranean lifestyle in which luxury, art and design blend together seamlessly.

Grand Hotel Central

Vía Layetana, 30
08003 Barcelona
El Born
Phone: +34 932 957 900
Fax: +34 932 681 215
www.grandhotelcentral.com

Price category: €€
Rooms: 147 rooms including suites
Facilities: "Actual Restaurant & Café", rooftop pool, gym
Services: Meeting rooms for up to 65 people
Located: next to Barcelona's cathedral, with spectacular views of the Gothic district and the ancient city walls
Public transportation: Metro Jaume I
Map: No. 12
Style: Contemporary design
What's special: Guests love this hotel for many reasons: for some it's the fashionable location in the heart of the El Born district, Las Ramblas, and the shopping zone around Plaza Catalunya, for others it's the spectacular infinity pool with the best view in the city, and still for others it's the food at "Actual Restaurant", but above all, it is the service that makes Grand Hotel Central so cool.

La Rambla, 109
(Entrance via Carrer Pintor Fortuny)
08002 Barcelona
Ciutat Vella
Phone: +34 935 529 552
Fax: +34 935 529 550
www.nnhotels.com
www.hotel1898.com

Price category: €€€€
Rooms: 169 rooms, 3 suites with terrace and pool
Facilities: Restaurant, library, outdoor heated pool, gym, solarium, spa with steam room, sauna and massages
Services: 5 conference rooms and business center
Located: in the heart of Barcelona at Las Ramblas
Public transportation: Metro Catalunya, Liceu
Map: No. 13
Style: Modern elements mixed with colonial atmosphere
What's special: Decorated in striking tones of red, white and black, the classical façade of the former headquarters of the Compañía General de Tabacos de Filipinas, hides a modern gem. Once inside, guests discover seven colonial meeting rooms, a fully equipped business center and a library. In addition, there is a full spa with gym and an outdoor swimming pool with solarium.

Hotel Omm

Rosselló, 265
08008 Barcelona
Eixample
Phone: +34 934 454 000
Fax: +34 934 454 004
www.hotelomm.es

Price category: €€€
Rooms: 91 rooms
Facilities: "Restaurant Moovida", "Restaurant Moo", "Ommsession Club", rooftop terrace with pool, spa
Services: 3 Meeting rooms
Located: in the heart of the city, right beside Passeig de Gràcia
Public transportation: Metro Diagonal
Map: No. 14
Style: Contemporary design
What's special: Omm is one of the hottest boutique hotels in the city and with good reason; the contemporary design coupled with "Restaurant Moo", make for an adventure in luxury lodging. Guests can savor views of Gaudí's La Pedrera from the roof top pool, or use the full spa.

Ejemplo

Phone: +34 934 816 767
Fax: +34 934 816 464
www.hotelpulitzer.es

Facilities: VISIT Restaurant", cocktail bar, easy food,
roof terrace, free access to "Holmes Place Fitness
Center"
Services: Free WiFi, room service, 24h concierge
Located: just a few minutes away from Las Ramblas and
Passeig de Gràcia
Public transportation: Metro Plaça Catalunya
Map: No. 15
Style: Boutique hotel
What's special: Pulitzer is a new hotel concept, where
light, a cool atmosphere and a cosmopolitan air win you
over. "VISIT Restaurant" fuses Mediterranean with subtle
oriental touches. It is situated in a converted greenhouse
which faces on to the delightful interior garden of the hotel

Hotel Soho Barcelona

Gran Vía, 543–545
08011 Barcelona
Eixample
Phone: +34 935 529 610
Fax: +34 935 529 611
www.hotelsohobarcelona.com

Price category: €
Rooms: 51 rooms
Facilities: Lounge, terrace, outdoor pool
Services: Conference room for up to 20 people
Located: next to Plaza Catalunya, Passeig de Gràcia, Las Ramblas, the Gothic district and the Cathedral
Public transportation: Metro Urgell, Universitat
Map: No. 16
Style: Contemporary design
What's special: As one of the most sophisticated hotels in all of Barcelona, Hotel Soho is a bit of downtown New York on the fabulous Gran Vía Avenue. Designed by Alfredo Arribas, this 51 room luxury boutique hotel is perfect for business and pleasure travelers alike. The roof top terrace and pool is a great place to spend a sunny afternoon.

Market Hotel

Passatge Sant Antoni Abat, 10
08015 Barcelona
Eixample
Phone: +34 933 251 205
Fax: +34 934 242 965
www.markethotel.com.es

Price category: €
Rooms: 46 rooms
Facilities: Restaurant, meeting room for 100 people
Services: Notebook available for guests, bicycle renting
Located: next to the San Antonio Market, between Plaza Catalunya and Plaza Espanya
Public transportation: Metro Sant Antoni and Urgell
Map: No. 17
Style: Modern
What's special: Named for a Barcelona landmark, the San Antonio Market, the first public market built outside the city walls, Market Hotel is an impossibly chic lodging option for the most fashionable customers. Each of the rooms in this comfortable boutique hotel is decorated in a minimal, Asian-inspired design scheme that exudes a Zen-like calm.

NERI Hotel & Restaurante

Carrer de Sant Sever, 5
08002 Barcelona
Ciutat Vella
Phone: +34 933 040 655
Fax: +34 933 040 637
www.hotelneri.com

Price category: €€
Rooms: 22 rooms
Facilities: Restaurant, lounge, bar, rooftop terrace, private meeting room, library, gothic terrace, Sensual Solarium
Services: Pillow and linen service, book & CD menu, Playstation, TFT TV, 24h room service, Neri&Beauty, personal shopper
Located: in the gothic district of Barcelona, next to the Cathedral and Sant Jaume Square
Public transportation: Metro Jaume I
Map: No. 18
Style: Contemporary design mixed with ancient influences
What's special: Located in a small 18th century palace, the NERI is comprised of just 22 rooms, each decorated according to the themes of each floor.

Alameda Mazarredo, 77
48009 Bilbao
País Vasco
Phone: +34 946 611 880
Fax: +34 944 255 182
www.mirohotelbilbao.com

Price category: €
Rooms: 50 rooms including 5 junior suites
Facilities: "Bar Miró", spa, hammam, jacuzzi, massage, library and art collection
Services: Conference rooms for up to 50 people
Located: between the Guggenheim and the Fine Arts Museum in Bilbao
Map: No. 19
Style: Contemporary urban style
What's special: Bilbao is one of the great destinations for art and design in the world, and now it has a luxury boutique hotel to match. Miró Hotel offers a quiet sophistication and unparalleled elegance located in the shadow of the Guggenheim Museum. Get drinks at "Bar Miró", get rubbed at the spa—there is something for everyone.

Hospes Villa Paulita

Avenida Pons i Gasch, 15
17520 Puigcerdà
Catalunya
Phone: +34 972 884 622
Fax: +34 972 884 632
www.hospes.com

Price category: €€
Rooms: 36 rooms and 2 suites
Facilities: Senzone "L'Estany" restaurant, Senzone fireplace bar. Bodyna massages & treatments, Bodyna indoor pool, Bodyna fitness area, dry and wet sauna
Services: Meeting rooms for up to 120 people
Located: directly at Lake of Puigcerdà in the center of the pyrenean village, 160 km to Barcelona airport and 180 km to Toulouse airport
Map: No. 20
Style: Neoclassic with a notable French influence
What's special: Once owned by an aristocratic family, the Villa Paulita is among the crown jewels of the Pyrenées. Though there are 36 rooms, it is the two luxury suites that are not to be missed. Glass pyramids throughout the gardens provide natural light to the underground Bodyna Spa

Mas de Torrent Hotel & Spa

Afores s/n
17123 Torrent, Girona
Catalunya
Phone: +34 902 550 321
Fax: +34 972 303 293
www.mastorrent.com

Price category: €€€
Rooms: 3 double rooms, 7 suites, 7 deluxe suites and 22 bungalows
Facilities: 2 restaurants, swimming pool, spa
Services: Nursery and amusements for children in summer, babysitter on request
Located: in the heart of El Baix Empordà, only a few kilometers away from the beach, near to the mediaeval villages of Pals and Peratallada
Map: No. 21
Style: Cottage house
What's special: Mas de Torrent was once an old traditional Catalan country home. Mas Spa features a traditional Turkish hammam, a heated swimming pool, and treatment rooms for men and women with heated marble tables.

Hospes Amérigo

Rafael Altamira, 7
03002 Alicante
Comunidad Valenciana
Phone: +34 965 146 570
Fax: +34 965 146 571
www.hospes.com

Price category: €
Rooms: 80 rooms including 1 superior suite
Facilities: Senzone restaurant, bar, lounge, tapas bar, rooftop lounge, Bodyna spa & wellness
Services: 12 meeting rooms for up to 200 people, "Way to sleep" service
Located: in the historical city center of Alicante, 10 km to El Altet airport
Map: No. 22
Style: Contemporary interior in an ancient convent
What's special: Located in the historical city center in a renovated Dominican convent, Hospes Amérigo is the chicest hotel in the region. A clash of old world and new the hotel features two restaurants, including tapas bar Senzone, two lounges, a rooftop swimming pool and a full service spa and wellness center, Bodyna.

Hospedería de La Parra

Santa María, 16
06176 La Parra
Extremadura
Phone: +34 924 682 692
Fax: +34 924 682 619
www.laparra.net

Price category: €
Rooms: 19 rooms and 2 suites
Facilities: Restaurant, swimming pool
Located: in a little village, 2,5-hours drive from Lisbon and 2-hours drive to the north of Sevilla
Map: No. 23
Style: Modern countrystyle
What's special: La Parra offers guests nothing less than an escape from the stresses of the modern world. There are no televisions, radios or air conditioning; instead the hotel exudes an air of peace and tranquility in every room. Built in a 17th century cloister, it is among the most relaxing spots in the world.

El Hotel Pacha

Paseo Marítimo s/n
07800 Ibiza
Islas Baleares
Phone: +34 971 315 963
Fax: +34 971 310 253
www.elhotelpacha.com

Price category: €€
Rooms: 57 suites
Facilities: Jacuzzi, indoor swimming pool
Located: on Paseo Maritimo, opposite to "Pacha Night club", in the heart of Ibiza
Map: No. 24
Style: Contemporary design
What's special: This chic, minimalist hotel is a respite from Ibiza's high energy lifestyle. Its small, contempora rooms are designed with pure relaxation in mind; each of the 57 suites are like islands of tranquility in a sea of chaos. Just five minutes from the Bay of Talamanca Hotel Pacha is perfectly situated.

Hotel Hacienda Na Xamena

Hotel Hacienda Na Xamena
07815 San Miguel, Ibiza
Islas Baleares
Phone: +34 971 334 500
Fax: +34 971 334 514
www.hotelhacienda-ibiza.com

Price category: €€€
Rooms: 65 rooms and suites
Facilities: 4 restaurants, fitness room, swimming pool spa & thalasso
Services: Private boats
Located: in the North West of the island
Map: No. 25
Style: Ibicenco & ethnic
What's special: Hacienda is "the Hotel Glamour" you have been dreaming of and where you will live very ma[ny] moments. One of the best vistas in all of Ibiza in one c[f] the island's most private settings. Though just 20 min[minutes] outside the city, the acres of pine forest and strik[ing] coastal scenery provide the perfect backdrop for this h[id]den jewel. Private chauffeur is available by reservation

C/Valladolid, 1–3
07839 S.Agustí des Vedrà, Ibiza
Islas Baleares
Phone: +34 971 345 000
Fax: +34 971 346 289
www.sespitreras.com

Price category: €€€
Rooms: 7 rooms
Facilities: Restaurant, pool bar, swimming pool, sauna, spa, turkish hammam
Located: in the town limits of Sant Josep, 12 km to the airport and 10-minutes drive to Ibiza town
Map: No. 26
Style: Luxurious
What's special: Containing only seven rooms, Ses Pitreras is an exclusive, and luxurious lodging option. The restaurant is known for its fresh local ingredients, and is a popular meeting spot for beautiful locals and visitors alike. The spa has one of only a few Turkish hammams on the island.

Hotel Marques de Riscal, The Luxury Collection

Calle Torrea, 1
01340 Elciego (Alava)
La Rioja
Phone: +34 945 180 880
Fax: +34 945 180 881
www.luxurycollection.com/
marquesderiscal

Price category: €€€€
Rooms: 43 rooms, including 10 suites
Facilities: 2 restaurants, winebar, rooftop lounge, wine cellar, library, pool, winetherapy spa and fitness center
Services: Babysitting service, mountain bikes with baby seats, quads rental & horse riding
Located: Marqués de Riscal's "City of Wine" is located in the medieval city Elciego in the wine-growing region La Rioja
Map: No. 27
Style: Minimalistic
What's special: This striking hotel is renowned architect Frank O. Gehry's second masterpiece in the heart of Spain. Managed by Starwood Hotels&Resorts, this small elegant gem has two gourmet restaurants and the "Caudalíe Vinothérapie Spa" in which all of the products are grape extracts and mineral water.

De Las Letras Hotel & Restaurante

Gran Vía, 11
28013 Madrid
Centro
Phone: +34 915 237 980
Fax: +34 915 237 981
www.hoteldelasletras.com

Price category: €€
Rooms: 102 rooms including 3 suites
Facilities: Restaurant, lounge, fitness & spa, solarium library
Services: Meeting rooms for up to 150 people
Located: in the city center next to the Puerta del Sol a Mayor Square
Public transportation: Metro Gran Vía, Sevilla
Map: No. 28
Style: Modern
What's special: All of the 103 rooms in this magical hotel are decorated according to the elegant, minimali palette of the central lobby. The three suites are two-s ried, and built under the spectacular domes that crown the building.

Hotel Silken Puerta América

Avenida de América, 41
28002 Madrid
Prosperidad District
Phone: +34 917 445 400
Fax: +34 917 445 401
www.hotelpuertamerica.com

Price category: €€€
Rooms: 327 rooms
Facilities: Restaurant, bars and café, garden, indoor swimming pool, sauna, business center
Services: Babysitting
Located: 8 km to Madrid-Barajas airport, in a business and commercial area of Madrid
Public transportation: Cartagena Metro
Map: No. 29
Style: Contemporary Design
What's special: Each of the 12 floors, the terrace and the parking, in this landmark hotel, has been designed by a world famous contemporary architect, including Zaha Hadid and Sir Norman Foster. The in house restaurant, "Lágrimas Negras", serves contemporary cuisine in a setting designed by Christian Liaigre.

Hotel Urban

Carrera de San Jerónimo, 34
28014 Madrid
Distrito de las Letras
Phone: +34 917 877 770
Fax: +34 917 877 799
www.derbyhotels.com

Price category: €€€
Rooms: 96 rooms
Facilities: Gourmet restaurant "Europa Decó" and "La Terraza", the "GlassBar", rooftop pool, solarium, art collection
Services: Meeting rooms
Located: in the cultural center of Madrid, next to the shopping and business district
Public transportation: Metro Sevilla
Map: No. 30
Style: Decó
What's special: One step into the soaring glass enclosed lobby and you're transported to another world in which old and new collide, creating a lodging concept for the 21st century. The hotel features a swimming pool, several restaurants and bars, and meeting spaces for large groups.

Santo Mauro

Calle de Zurbano, 36
28010 Madrid
Chamberi
Phone: +34 913 196 900
Fax: +34 913 085 477
www.hotelacsantomauro.com

Price category: €€€
Rooms: 51 rooms and suites
Facilities: "Santo Mauro Restaurant", lobby bar, indoor pool, garden, fitness center
Services: Butler service, meeting rooms
Located: in the center of Madrid, close to Paseo de la Castellana
Public transportation: Metro Ruben Darío, Alonso Martínez
Map: No. 31
Style: Elegant
What's special: Originally built for the Duke of Santo Mauro in 1894, the building is one of the finest palaces in Madrid. The original library has been converted into the incredible "Santo Mauro Restaurant".

Hospes Maricel

Carretera d'Andratx, 11
07184 Calvià, Mallorca
Islas Baleares
Phone: +34 971 707 744
Fax: +34 971 707 745
www.hospes.com

Price category: €€€
Rooms: 29 rooms
Facilities: Senzone restaurant, Senzone cocktail bar, pool
Services: Meeting rooms
Located: on the Mediterranean beach side, close to Palma de Mallorca, 20 km to Palma airport
Map: No. 32
Style: Artistic elegance
What's special: This small seaside boutique property is among the best places to watch the famous Mallorcan sunsets. Guests can enjoy one of several signature massage therapies in stone caves by the Mediterranean Sea

Portixol

Calle Sirena, 27
07006 Palma de Mallorca,
Mallorca
Islas Baleares
Phone: +34 971 271 800
Fax: +34 971 275 025
www.portixol.com

Price category: €€
Rooms: 26 rooms, 13 of them with terrace
Facilities: Restaurant, bar, pool, spa, conference room
Services: 24 hours all year round
Located: just outside Palma de Mallorca, directly at Portixol port
Map: No. 33
Style: Mediterranean and Scandinavian mixture
What's special: Open since 1956, but recently transformed into a luxury destination, the Portixol features a full service restaurant, bar and rooms decorated in simple, Scandinavian style. The seaside lunch is an elegant way to enjoy the freshest lobster on the island.

Puro

Monte Negro, 12
07012 Palma de Mallorca,
Mallorca
Islas Baleares
Phone: +34 971 425 450
Fax: +34 971 425 451
www.purohotel.com

Price category: €
Rooms: 26 rooms and suites
Facilities: "Opio Bar & Restaurant", patios, rooftop terrace, plunge pool, 10-minutes drive to beach club
Services: Babysitting, concierge, personal shopper, massages
Located: in Palma's old town La Lonja, next to the historic and shopping districts of Palma
Map: No. 34
Style: Urban casual chic for global nomad travelers
What's special: Condé Nast Traveller named Puro one of its hottest hotels in the world in 2005. "Opio Restaurant" is a popular spot for locals and visitors not only due to the Mediterranean cuisine, but the nightly DJ spinning ambient and house seven nights a week.

Son Brull Hotel & Spa

Crta. Palma-Pollensa, km 50
07460 Pollensa, Mallorca
Islas Baleares
Phone: +34 971 535 353
Fax: +34 971 531 068
www.sonbrull.com

Price category: €€
Rooms: 16 rooms and 7 suites
Facilities: "Restaurant 3|65", bar, terrace, 2 swimming pools
Services: Free use of the spa areas, WiFi in the whole hotel, bicycles
Located: in the North of the island, 55 km to Palma airport
Map: No. 35
Style: Modern, design-oriented luxury hotel
What's special: Tucked away in an ancient olive tree grove, Son Brull's spa is a must-visit. Using only natural ingredients, guests receive special treatments using olive oil. During some months, guests receive use of a free car during their stay.

Son Gener

Ctra viera Son Servera
Arta, km. 3
07550 Son Servera, Mallorca
Islas Baleares
Phone: +34 971 183 612/736
Fax: +34 871 706 016
www.songener.com

Price category: €€
Rooms: 10 rooms
Facilities: Swimming pools, spa, sauna and hamman
Services: Breakfast and dinner
Located: in the East of the island between Son Server
and Arta
Map: No. 36
Style: Modern countrystyle
What's special: Organic gardens give way to sweeping
views of the surrounding countryside at Son Gener. Bu
almost entirely of limestone, the interior spaces are a
once cool and modern, and inviting. Indoor and outdoc
swimming pools provide year round fun.

The Beach House

Urb: El Chaparral
CN. 340 km 203
29648 Mijas Costa, Marbella
Andalucía
Phone: +34 952 494 540
Fax: +34 952 494 540
www.beachhouse.nu

Price category: €
Rooms: 10 rooms
Facilities: Bar, lounge, heated pool
Services: Conference room
Located: directly on the beach between Málaga and Marbella on the outskirts of the village of La Cala, 20 minutes drive to Málaga airport
Map: No. 37
Style: Cool elegance
What's special: This private pension located directly on the water is an unparalleled romantic destination. The pool is heated year round.

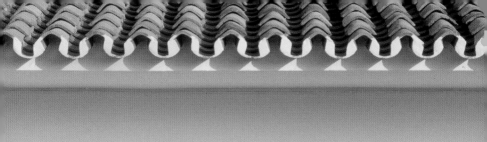

Hotel San Roque

Calle Esteban de Ponte, 32
38450 Garachico, Isla Baja,
Tenerife
Islas Canarias
Phone: +34 922 133 435
Fax: +34 922 133 406
www.hotelsanroque.com

Price category: €€
Rooms: 20 rooms including 4 suites
Facilities: "Anturium Restaurant", "Hoffmann Bar", swimming pools
Services: Meeting rooms
Located: in the center of Garachico, a short distance to the old port
Map: No. 38
Style: Boutique hotel
What's special: This striking red hotel is an unusual mixture of traditional 17th century classical architecture and modern Bauhaus-style design. The main courtyard contains a heated swimming pool.

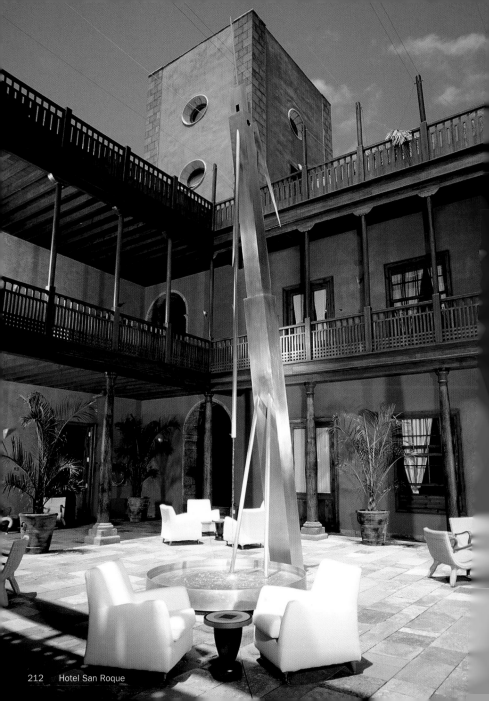

Hospes Palau de la Mar

Navarro Reverter, 14
46004 Valencia
Comunidad Valenciana
Phone: +34 963 162 884
Fax: +34 963 162 885
www.hospes.com

Price category: €€
Rooms: 66 rooms including 1 Presidential Suite
Facilities: Senzone restaurant, Senzone lounge & cocktail bar, Bodyna massages & treatments, Bodyna jacuzzi pool, Bodyna sauna and turkish bath, Bodyna fitness
Services: Meeting rooms for up to 200 people
Located: in the fashionable area of Valencia, 10 km to Manises airport
Public transportation: Metro Alameda and Colón
Map: No. 39
Style: 19th century baronial mansion
What's special: The cool, clean lines of the modern interior provide a stark contrast to the traditional façade. The hotel's inner patio is a popular place to relax while bathed in the famous Spanish sunlight.

Santiago de Compostela

Badajoz

23

Sev

5

Cadiz

38

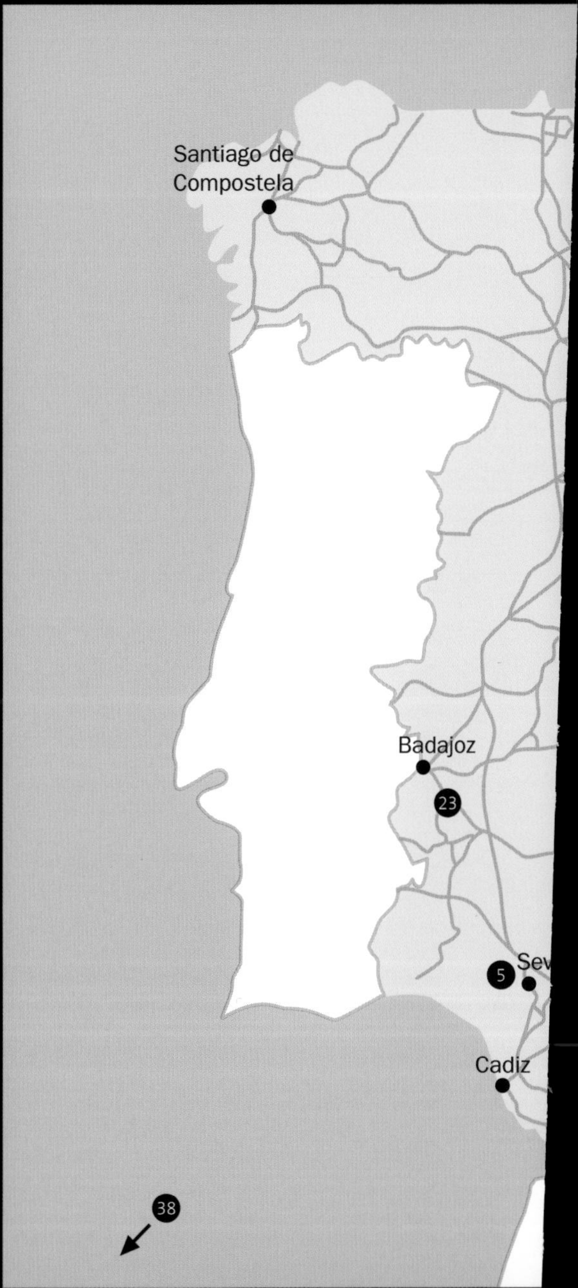

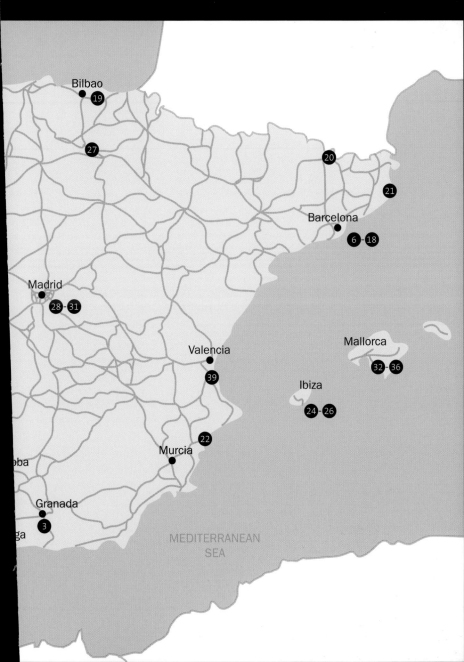

Other titles by teNeues

Styleguides

ISBN 978-3-8327-9206-0

ISBN 978-3-8327-9207-7

ISBN 978-3-8327-9205-3

ISBN 978-3-8327-9234-3

ISBN 978-3-8327-9230-5

ISBN 978-3-8327-9243-5

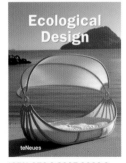

ISBN 978-3-8327-9229-9

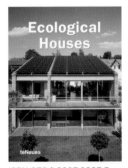

ISBN 978-3-8327-9227-5

ISBN 978-3-8327-9228-2

Size: **15 x 19 cm**, 6 x 7 ½ in., 224 pp., **Flexicover**, c. 280 color photographs,
Text: English / German / French / Spanish / Italian

www.teneues.com

Other titles by teNeues

Cool Hotels

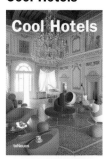

ISBN 978-3-8327-9105-6

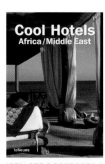

ISBN 978-3-8327-9051-6

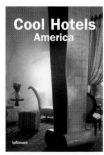

ISBN 978-3-8238-4565-2

ISBN 978-3-8327-9134-6

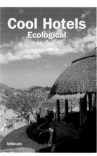

ISBN 978-3-8327-9135-3

ISBN 978-3-8327-9203-9

Size: **13.5 x 19 cm**, 5 ¼ x 7 ½ in., 400 pp., **Flexicover**, c. 400 color photographs,
Text: English / German / French / Spanish / Italian

Cool Restaurants

ISBN 978-3-8238-4585-0

ISBN 978-3-8327-9103-2

ISBN 978-3-8327-9146-9

Size: **14.6 x 22.5 cm**, 5 ¾ x 8 ¾ in., 136 pp., **Flexicover**, c. 130 color photographs,
Text: English / German / French / Spanish / Italian
www.teneues.com

Other titles by teNeues

Cool Restaurants

ISBN 978-3-8327-9118-6

ISBN 978-3-8327-9066-0

ISBN 978-3-8327-9147-6

ISBN 978-3-8327-9232-9

ISBN 978-3-8327-9068-4

ISBN 978-3-8327-9067-7

Cool Spots

ISBN 978-3-8327-9154-4

ISBN 978-3-8327-9152-0

ISBN 978-3-8327-9177-3

Size: **14.6 x 22.5 cm**, 5 ³/₄ x 8 ³/₄ in., 136 pp., **Flexicover**, c. 130 color photographs,
Text: English / German / French / Spanish / Italian
www.teneues.com